FORGIVE
The Unforgivable

FORGIVE
The Unforgivable

Taking My Life Back

DESIREE DUVALL

I want to thank my sons, family and friends,
for their unwavering support.
To all of you who believed in me
and encouraged me to write another book
and be part of the solution about forgiving.
I'm deeply grateful.

TABLE OF CONTENTS

PROLOGUE

⚛

orgive the unforgivable was written to help others identify answers to the obstacles many of us face with forgiveness. In my case it was overcoming the trauma of a tumultuous marriage and divorce in order to be free for the brilliant life that was held hostage. That the rage and hate caused by malicious, vile and evil actions could somehow turn into heartfelt, true compassion seemed incomprehensible. Learning how to forgive the unforgivable acts of not just one individual, but several other people that I allowed unknowingly to hurt me through the years, was one of the final steps to taking my life back and achieving true happiness. And to do so required small steps and quiet moments of healing.

I was encouraged by those close to me to share my analogies and encouragement to other people, looking for guidance and answers on how to move forward and accept the unpleasant truth as I did. People are never going to ever change because we asked them to; we must alter our own behavior to make the transformation for a better existence, period. Being absolved leaves no one to blame; it means complete forgiveness.

The core of the human soul is the heart. A complete change of heart can heal just about anything. Forgiving the unforgivable will enable people to take a closer look at how to deal with forgiveness and find a way to move on with life, specific to their own situation. A sense of power filled with great joy brings satisfaction that can no longer be affected by outside opinion. To be forgiving means forgiving the abuser and yourself no matter what. Forgiveness is a fundamental part of being Christian, as well as an immense feeling of solace in the liberation of self. Freedom comes when we forgive by allowing us to fully be who we are in love.

Having been involved in multiple abusive and toxic relationships both personal and professional, I needed to find out why I continued to find these types of relationships and how to build healthier ones. At first those relationships made me happy, as I felt safe and needed, but in later years those same experiences made me feel unsatisfied, defenseless, and unimportant, because they were not healthy and I had grown to want more for myself. I was attracted to the same dysfunction I once knew as a child so was reacting out of conditioning rather than acting from my true thoughts and values. Different people and experiences, but the feeling of being drawn in was the same.

Ever heard of the expression, my biology is my biography? That was me. I spent time around others with broken marriages, family dealing with their own anxiety/health issues; friends and co-workers hiding behind a persona that they were somehow better than most because they had money, even though that money was acquired from their parents. No one was driven and no one was making a difference for humanity, as they were all self-serving. I was disgusted. It went against my grain and faith.

It was all a lie and I wanted out and nothing to do with these toxic relationships. Living a lie, I was unable to speak out and take control of my very breath. Unfortunately I felt powerless, desperate and depressed, faced with the challenge of recovering my courage and confronting all offenders that abused my immediate family and myself during and after my marriage. What I was seeing, feeling and experiencing was ugly and despite what other's believed or heard through mere gossip, I did the right thing by keeping silent and walking away. It was because I believe anyone who's first to run their mouth is usually the guilty one, as they are hiding something, that I continued steadfast in my silence. Unbelievably, I was personally challenged for remaining quiet and dealing with rumors that were unfairly justified. This type of behavior is that of a coward, moving the attention so they wouldn't be exposed for their wrong doings.

Sometimes doing what is so hard and at times may feel wrong, is actually the right thing to do. I did what I did for the respect of my children and me. It was time to end the dead-end relationship(s) in my life. It serves no point to be bitter—just let the suffering end and relieve myself of those that brought harm from further obligation. This is the true reason for forgiveness and one of the most difficult aspects as well, especially considering forgiveness of self.

Also, when anyone interferes in someone else's family's pain, it's very disrespectful, damaging and considered selfish. I could spend the rest of my life wondering why, but what's the point. I could see there was deeper pain in these people beyond me. My life was just foreplay to them; they are people with low self-esteem and on all accounts abusers too. To live a healthy life in line with your passion, it is very vital to forgive them even if the hurt was intentional. It doesn't do anyone good by hanging on to old insulting memories. Whether or not these people change, it doesn't matter as the damage has been done, time to move on and not digress one day longer on the injustices that occurred.

Dwelling on the abuse only gives power to the abuser and takes away our ability to see a positive future. We all deserve a better life filled with promise, honest people and great love. No more deception, no more pretending to be happy and dissatisfied. It's never easy to walk away from the life we once had, even a toxic one. Wanting a life to mean something more and live without the misery, regret or to always be worried. My personal relationships changed immensely because my children and I experienced a new form of love that was earned rather than expected, and it came with no conditions. We have a unique bond that is priceless.

Forgive the Unforgivable is a wakeful reminder of oneness —one woman's courage to seek personal answers, despite all obstacles. By processing, sharing and forgiving, moving on takes place and provides a path through forgiveness to a passionate, truly happy existence. The power of not being angry, instead being able to help others overcome and providing ways of moving on are reasons I wrote this. These steps take careful thought and benefit from journaling questions and answers, thoughts and concerns. Take the time to work through the negativity and change to feelings and beliefs that are beneficial to your values and expectations of self. Always advocating the truth, the value of family, healthy relationships and my belief in the heavenly father.

Times when it's imperative to bounce back regardless of the challenge require a drive and a dream of something better. Life can't be lived if all you do is make excuses and bring blame. Haven't we all seen enough of that? Time is so important, as we can't get it back. Understanding what we can do to make our life better by admission, and getting past the heartache, takes careful thought and pushing through uncomfortable barriers. Sometimes the answers are brutally hard to accept because forgiving is too hard. No one ever said you had to forget.

When you are ready, able, fully conscious and inspired, imagine how courageous anyone can be because they dared to let go, move on, and forgive the unforgivable, even ourselves. This is very empowering for any man, woman or child no matter their circumstances. Imagine if we could truly be more than we know and life could be fuller? Letting someone off the hook by telling him or her you're sorry they fell in love with you can break you free from the resentment you hold inside. Similarly, forgiving a betrayal of any kind allows you to break through the bitterness and find peace.

Devastation brings complexities and the courage to let those issues go takes careful thought of planning and time. If you don't already, now would be a good time to start believing in the phenomena of miracles and the ability to create a comfortable life filled with great joy. You must believe you are worthy without validation from anyone else. We are all suitable for change, but many of us will not try, because it's super hard and scary. And many don't like change or simply they don't have the courage to be different or admit something is wrong. For the rest of us, although we've made incredible drive towards equality, we are still somehow wrestling with feelings and those emotions interfere our reassurance and confirmation about our person. Staying in what we know is easy and comfortable. Even if it is an abusive situation, or one not in alignment with who we want to be, it is often easier to stay because it is familiar and might even be considered secure as it is the known. Believing can be difficult and at times feels impossible.

If we can position ourselves better for valor maybe we can help our psychological ability. This all stems from a mature perspective and consideration to what is in align with the values we have for our self. Digging deep within our conscious minds and exploring the inner you usually can't be done unless there is some sort of forgiveness with self. It's never easy to discard deficiencies or minor failures. Who likes fault right? It is a tough process to realize and fight to change things inside ourselves that are contrary to our beliefs and ideals. However doing so unleashes great power within. Locating our power within helps us to identify our capacity, which empowers ourselves and influences others.

Having the authority to act, capacity to do something with persuasive skill, energy to drive with force and ability to reject any idea because you say so is supremacy. You will never feel vulnerable again and peace will be with you no matter what you're dealing with. The gift of strength is emotional toughness, resistance and having a defensive ability. Bottom line is persuasive power and who doesn't want that as an asset or quality? We can never prepare enough when we lose someone special in marriage, relationship or in death, so we must conquer the situation voluntarily and surrender to faith and our heavenly father. This is where the strength is, the strength that builds our ability to defend ourselves and the power to persevere. Otherwise you will be defeated and the pain will become unsurmountable and wear you down.

Despite the many obstacles we face daily we all know the adverse effects of conflict. Stop being stubborn, refusing to change and let go of control. Confront resistance and break through barriers. It's about obstinacy. Perhaps we struggle with reservations and the uncertainties of letting go because after all, it's a frightening thought of more worries of anxiety to come. Or is this just the beginning of the change we need and not allowing adversity to get in the way of your dreams. We all have experienced the feeling of incredible; meaning great, wonderful and fabulous. All are pleasing feelings, but when we challenge the things in our life that bring hurt, fear, and guilt or conflict and dispute we sometimes encounter resistance. For us to find true happiness we need to free our hearts, mind and soul. In order to worship our life it takes personal integrity, respect, dignity in the highest position and redressing your reputation.

Our sorrows are the continuation of persisting behavior; these never ending feelings can be genuine, faithful, in-tune and aware not only of physical existing, but they are verifiable, undisputed. By breaking through these sorrows, using the ten tools to help you move on, or other tips in this book, you can find freedom. Naturally the freedom from conflict is finding your happy place and the mental aptitude to love once more. The key to have courage to change is to have physical power, emotional toughness, resistance, and defensive ability. Listen to yourself for you and only you have your answers. So listen to your intuition and claim your life back on your terms.

It is always difficult to understand and appreciate the courage it takes to acknowledge your powers and set boundaries. Too often we are much too tired and if we push the limit we may find ourselves physically or mentally sick or better yet angry, as we are not always able to please everyone. Possibly if we spent more time being authentic and frank and establishing respectable boundaries we would be less likely to hurt others or ourselves.

I hope this book offers the supportive foundation you need to find answers moving onward, forgiving the unforgivable. If you want more information about my story and how I got to forgiveness please read *Letting Go: Surrendering My Heart to God.* As we progress together through this book we will focus on moving towards forgiveness (of ourselves and others) to the ultimate goal of pure happiness. Learning as we go that it is possible and in your best interest to forgive the unforgivable.

With love and blessings,

Desiree.

POWER

Grace: Take Your Lumps

In times of difficulty or absurd and negative circumstances, it is easy to rage against injustice. Although it may be difficult, believing in the power to overcome and acting with grace will allow peace, balance and comprehension to be revealed. Instead of focusing on the injustice of what happen, believe you will learn from it and move on. To learn how to accept difficulties that cross our paths, to take our lumps as part of the amazing journey we are on, is an incredible feat of faith.

> **(New International Version, Gen. 3:15)**
> *I will walk by faith even when I cannot walk.*
> 2 Corinthians 57

All too often life deals all of us difficult circumstances where we want answers now and everything to be done and put to bed right away. Unfortunately as we all know it doesn't necessarily work that way. We need to take each situation and break it down, mess by mess. Our quandary is it's extremely tiresome and annoying. When we are baffled with life and I'll be the first to exclaim that certain aspects that go along with daily life can be so at baffling times, it is easy to begin to feel dejected. Naturally we try to figure out the answers by ourselves or we ask for guidance from close and dear family and friends. The goal is to resolve the problem and we will do whatever we need to do to make that happen. Divide and conquer as they say and that's what we do. Starting by breaking it down into small bite size pieces and take on what you can hourly, day-by-day or week-by-week and it will get done and resolved. Never ever allow yourself to be inundated, overwhelmed, or forlorn. Forgive yourself that you don't have all the information, or the time, or other requirements needed to alleviate the situation. All you have is today and tomorrow there will be more. Through it all, in our graceful belief in the power of love, our faith brings us to forgiveness. Rest assured, if you come to peace with yourself, it will be easy to let go and forgive others that have brought you any sadness or difficult situations.

Breaking Habits

Too often we leap in to the rescue when we see the first sign of panic. Perhaps mothers have this tendency more as we are hardwired to nurture and often do not realize that people do not always need to be saved. Whoever told us we have to rescue everyone? Reality tells us that it is impossible, because no one knows for sure what the other party needs to be happy only they know that. We are not here to jump in and save people from their journey but when we are used to jumping in to prevent negative outcomes, it becomes a habit.

Nevertheless this is a bad habit that is hard to break, because we want to help, as we are rescuers by nature. We need to re-train our minds that everyone in this world must find their own way, because no one can do it for you. The hardest thing can be stepping back and watching people we love make mistakes, especially when we see it happening and the person involved does not. We need to remember we have been in their shoes and need to learn, in our time and the way that is right for us.

Other habits that ought to be broken include taking the easy way out, instead of doing the work ourselves, for ourselves, being dependent on others and not taking time for ourselves. In these cases, we believe other people or societal perceptions about who we are or should be. It can be difficult to break the habit of be-lieving what we are told and focusing on who we are and how we will move forward. Dependency is another habit that needs to be realized before it can be broken. When forgiving and moving away from negative people we often do not realize we are depen-dent on them. We come to rely on these people, however abusive, to form our beliefs about ourselves. Before we can forgive we must break the habit of dependency and fully rely on ourselves.

The Power to Say No

No is a very powerful and expensive word. What in the world tells us to say yes when we want to say no? We know we should. We are afraid of what someone will think of us if we don't do what he or she wants. Why are we afraid of disappointing others so much? When we feel the right to say no, and say it with full consciousness, people usually think it's just fine. We often find that when we expect others to accept our opinion and to respect our boundaries, they generally do. So we need to respect our self and pay attention to ourselves, and to say no more often, especially when we mean it.

This power to say no begins to develop when we make the decision to let go of negative people or situations in our life but it must be practiced to become dominant. It takes time to build confidence within ourselves to be able to have the power to say no. With time, self-exploration and practice, the power to say no will free us from the individuals and experiences that are not beneficial to our healing or are intolerable and inexcusable.

Confronting Distress

When we investigate our moods, we are examining our feelings and attitudes. When confronting distress we need to look down the throat of the monster that handicaps us. Plain and simple our temper debilitates our opportunities to be happy and successful and we do it to ourselves every day. The goal to advance our development requires us to be diligent in letting go of past feelings of impairment and rejections. In order to move forward and not stay stagnant and irritable we need to acknowledge our hurts and find it in our heart to forgive ourselves for any past and future emotional distress.

Confronting distress leads to forgiveness. This forgiveness includes emotional outbursts or reactions we experience that are not in line with our belief system or where we want to be. In this instance our faith reminds us to keep moving forward instead of dwelling in negative emotion or irritability. By acknowledging and facing head on the challenges, situations and people that are causing us the most distress and holding us back in ways we have not even realized yet, we can provide ourselves with an opportunity to see at face value the reality of the hurt. This paves the way for moving forward.

Why We Can

Those that say they can usually don't limit themselves to ambitious and wishful thinking. Knowing what they want to achieve, they go for it. It is common to have the courage for what it takes forming thoughts, but most lack the ability to see it through because they stall with excuses.

Putting something off until later will only make you late to the game of life and it can also give you a reputation as a procrastinator. Rather than defer any longer, find the confidence within you and make that first fearless step, be adventurous because after all, you have the assurance and the pledge of control to yourself of a positive "You Can" attitude.

Once you have found your passion, your reason to be, you must take action to initiate the life of your making. You can because you will. Keep that knowledge close to your heart and take action daily to move towards your passion. The life you want can become attainable through belief, and constant actions. Start by knowing you can accomplish anything no matter how big or seemingly unachievable. Then move forward constantly remembering that you can and will achieve the life of your dreams.

Avoiding Despair

How do we avoid despair? Obvious answer is don't bring it into your life, right? Easier said than done. Every day you enter the possibility of endangering yourself or others foolishly and unknowingly. Every day we all run chances that something will go wrong, and invite bad consequences without knowing. That risk involves the possibility of injury, damage or harm in a wide variety of forms and outcomes.

The truth of the matter is there are no guarantees in life and unless we take some risks, your life will be limited and sheltered. Faith in our ability to succeed even when risks are high is a mix of courage and belief. This way we allow forgiveness and comprehension and avoid despair.

Even when we know we can do something, we will experience moments of frustration and despair. Not everything will come easily and even things we are passionate about will have bumps in the road to success. It can be difficult not to feel despair and want to give up when things become challenging or we face a roadblock. Instead of feeling despair we must rise to the challenge and persevere. The path to a life of happiness, fulfilling exactly what you dream you can do, is full of risks and uncertainty.

Taking the courage to run those risks without fear of how or why they will be overcome and without considering external malice is an intelligent way to avoid despair. Of course each action step, each small move toward the people and things you want, needs to be considered. It's very crucial to review your thinking and whom and what you are getting involved with before you step out of your comfort zone. Sometimes people are not who they say they are, and they will hurt you without known cause. Be cautious with your time and protect your heart from pain.

Wanting More

To desire more in life is noble. When you are true to yourself and truly forgive you learn about your personal interests, passions and goals, subsequently wanting more than your current life offers. Making a deliberate decision to act on those options takes courage and forgiveness of preconception of others from past experiences and relationships. It is a positive step in the right direction to want more.

Sometimes it is enough to want more, without knowing exactly what that means. Often, especially at the depth of despair, we only know that our current situation is crushing us. The small inclination that we will not allow this (whatever it may be) to break us and that we can move forward is plenty. It is the birthplace of hope, the knowledge that through faith we can become what we are meant to be even if we have no idea what that is right now. The act of wanting more is the beginning of forgiveness.

Forgiveness is the fragrance that the violet sheds on the heel that has crushed it.

Mark Twain

By believing in more for ourselves and beginning the process of forgiving, a new perspective begins. Having the right perspective points to something whether actuality or truth. This registers measurement about what someone thinks or intends should be done in order to be happier. Allowing belief in self to override other people's assumptions moves us toward the life we seek. The choice is yours.

Being impartial from public opinion is being selfish for you.

Give yourself permission to let go of the tangled web you lived and ask for more, it's ok to take a chance. Focus on the positive things you want to achieve rather than the negative things others have said or taught you to believe. Let go of the anger and hurt and hold onto what you want for yourself. It may after all improve your life.

Breaking the Cycle

When ending the cycle of conflict someone has to take responsibility for the relationship. Someone has to stop playing the game. If you want to end the conflict, you need to stop resisting and end the torment by apologizing, and forgiving the other person. It is also essential to begin the examination of forgiveness of self because you love yourself enough to say no more. This removes the other person's resistance towards you and their ability to influence your life.

This is what it is meant to clear up the past and let the other one know you're playing a different game now. Instead of living in the conflict we are taking the opportunity to make changes to improve our lives. We are letting go of a negative game, a cycle with no end by forgiving them and removing ourselves from the situation. By giving THEM freedom, we take away the need to resist. Then the focus can be placed on you, so you won't miss your opportunity, one human being to another.

Breaking the cycle can be more difficult in some cases than others. In extreme situations it is not one simple choice. When breaking the cycle means confronting conflict in all aspects of your life the very thought of it is daunting. For me personally I couldn't break the cycle, I couldn't move forward towards forgiveness until my complete surrender. Every aspect of my life was connected to the cycle of destruction. Without a complete breakdown and consequential leap of faith, the task was too monumental to consider. It is important not to underestimate the severity of the situation you are in now. In my case I had to walk away to survive.

Ending the cycle is imperative; of course this action is not as simple as the words used to describe it. Breaking the cycle requires a faith that is stronger than the cycle of conflict that has been built. By forgiving the conflict from both sides, even when it is still going on, it ends immediately and you can move forward with love toward what God intended for you. ✤

CONSCIOUSNESS

Personal Awareness

None enjoys the feeling of helplessness. But if we do not confront or accept our fears we will always wrestle with internal conflict and discern pain as the only outcome for our future. The simple truth, conflict is a mental struggle with courage, is overcome through awareness. Do we have what it takes to be different? And do you want to take the appropriate measures to be different because after all you're worth it. Being aware of who we are, how we are different and what passion we want to pursue is only possible with conscious practice.

Knowing oneself is based from experience whether being sensible, learned, and shrewd or disrespected; it all comes down to pointing your finger at yourself enough to move forward. Spending time re-learning and examining what you know allows true self, knowledge and passion to persevere. If we are focusing on conscious awareness, we are showing good sense of being practical, functional and fully us. That is what having courage is all about, because strength comes from utilizing all facets of the brain.

Having the assurance and the belief in our own abilities allows us to have faith, to ask for advice from someone when needed. No one said you ever had to do it alone. The people you trust can help you control that fight within you and gain a better understanding of the leadership you are looking for. It is important, in this case to be aware of what you need and be honest when seeking help so that the person providing advice or assistance is doing so in an unbiased way, rather than for their own agenda.

Being resourceful requires you to be new and original too. Escaping your insecurities only comes to those who have will power and fortitude, because they have found their firmness of purpose. Opening your awareness to your purpose helps progression and moving on by fixing our thoughts on a passionate plan for our life. In this way, awareness is an essential attribute of forgiveness.

Confession

Confession to our weaknesses can be powerful as it's the first step to acceptance. It can set yourself and someone else free physically, and provide a release from social constraints. Very empowering if you are contending with certain elements of depression and wanting the pain to stop. Acknowledging our fears and weaknesses and then forgiving ourselves to overcome them, allows us to unleash our passion without fear. After we have had the opportunity to confess our weaknesses and fears, we can forgive ourselves and move forward with love.

The initial steps of confession take time, patience and delving deep into our inner selves. Our weaknesses are not always clear to us and we may find ourselves making excuses for them. Honesty with self and prayer or meditation, to open ourselves up to confess our weaknesses, requires a resilience and strength of faith. True confession takes place in an environment preparing for self-forgiveness, a true desire to overcome weaknesses in anticipation for the life we are striving to lead. Write down your weaknesses, confessing honestly to yourself how they have held you back and how you can better move forward without them. Once again this can be achieved by starting small and focusing on the end result we hope to achieve. This confession provides a clean slate to move forward with positive goals.

If you were to take some time and concentrate on your goals, passions, accomplishments, events, or influences you have had on others, maybe then you will foster new fearless acts to support the positive aspects of your life. The movement from confession of weakness to moving forward in love and passion encourages positivity in your life, especially if you have children. You are leading by example, showing your children how to turn weakness, difficulty and strife into a passionate faith in the power of self. This is done by forgiving the unforgivable in self and others and will propel you into your new life.

Your new life requires defense and the ability to find your heart again. Take some time to evaluate what you have learned and what you love as well as what you don't want or will not tolerate again. Replacing the old, negative life with a new one in line with your consciousness allows you to live entirely in positive perseverance. Journal your thoughts and share them with someone who deeply cares for you. In sharing, there is an opportunity to examine weaknesses and discuss how to prevent repeat occurrences of resulting behavior. Letting go of anger, despair and excuses, especially when permitting someone in your life such a responsibility to view an intimate confession, is boldness. Such trust is valor, and that's what we need to give to others so we may receive the courage to forgive.

Attitude

Do you ever wonder why we let things, events, or comments fester? Why can't we overlook or move on quickly? Is it that we consent to others exploiting us so they may benefit once again from our pain? This only happens if you let it. Our attitude is a chosen reaction to our environment and external stimulus. This reaction is conditioned over time as a habitual reaction or bad attitude and can be particularly nasty when dealing with an abusive or combative person, relationship or situation.

While working in property management I had the opportunity to see people in varied relationships both positive and negative. This gave me the opportunity to view other combative people personally, professionally and from a distance. This perspective helped me learn to surrender to my faith and retain a positive attitude in all situations. By seeing how other people reacted and allowed their attitude to be affected by another individual was helpful in making the connection to my own life. People are constantly pulled into an argumentative situation of blame and guilt derived from the actions or words of another person. Not allowing other's negativity to permeate my truth, my life and my reality was an essential lesson learned over years of watching people relate.

Forgiveness is not an occasional act, it is a constant attitude.   Martin Luther King Jr.

Sometimes, guilt-ridden feelings appear because of another lingering matter. If our attitude has been affected by a relationship, we may have actions, words or experiences that we are not proud of. It is time to stop punishing yourself for the actions of others or being ashamed for past wrong doings. The past is over and you're not the same person any more. Letting go means just that. No longer are you to be punished for the acts of someone else, regardless of what is said or done. It really doesn't matter what anyone thinks or believes except what you think; your own personal truth.

Acceptance

It's up to you. What we want most is to have peace on our planet, peace in our lives and peace in our hearts. This is something we think we want, but we live in a way that makes this almost impossible. Competition, comparison and deriding differences are celebrated. Instead of being accepting and appreciative, we've been taught to be judgmental and critical. We make excuses by not taking responsibility for our lives, and we've been taught, we are programmed, to blame as well as to resent someone or something separate from ourselves.

Without ever knowing how or why we destroy love, both in our relationships and in our own lives by not being accepting of the challenges we face. Instead we pass judgement and point to other people's failures instead of accepting who they are and looking within ourselves. This creates resistance and opposition against us and is a roadblock to forgiveness. We create tremendous suffering, and none of it is necessary. It is possible to live in the experience of love and it is possible to have love in all your relationships and in every aspect of your life. However, to do this you need to adopt a new way of living.

You need to learn how to flow with life and to be more accepting and tolerant of others. Start to forgive and to heal your heart. Put your focus on the wellbeing of others and self-improvement. Have it be more important to be free inside than to win, to be right and to get what you want.

(NIV, Gen 3:15)

Judge not, that you be not judged. For with the judgment you pronounce you will be judged, and with the measure you use it will be measured to you. Why do you see the speck that is in your brother's eye, but do not notice the log that is in your own eye? Or how can you say to your brother, 'Let me take the speck out of your eye,' when there is the log in your own eye? You hypocrite, first take the log out of your own eye, and then you will see clearly to take the speck out of your brother's eye.

Matthew 7:1-5

Put your focus on finding solutions that work for everyone. Open your heart, express your love and find the forgiveness you need to move forward. You certainly can do any of this as soon as you forgive, accept and love yourself. When you live your life in this way, opposition melts. You create an environment of love and support. Life works for you instead of against you. This is the key to being effective in life, but to make this happen, you need to do some work. You need to be committed to creating a life of love. Remember, every time you interact with another person you will either create love or destroy love, and whatever you give will come right back. If your situation looks tough or seems impossible, don't quit. Keep giving love. Follow your intuition and keep taking the next step. Then take the next step and the next one. When it gets hard and you want to give in, or to quit, choose love. Keep your focus on the result you want and keep taking the next step. Eventually your situation will clear up. And you will be fine. The only thing that can get in your way is your pride and ego. You have a choice. You can either live out of your pride and go, or you can do what works. You are the one who has to live with the consequences of whatever you choose. It would be great if the other person would cooperate the same way, but we certainly do not have to wait for that. If you want your life to be great, you are the one who's going to make it happen. It's up to you when, where and how.

Awareness

The scope of awareness is having the courage to say no and not take on any one issue or drama. You may have enough of your own. The more we carry on, the more we become involved, and we don't want that if we are in search of a better life. Finding the voice required to say no more often to other people's drama is the day you hold the key to your power of awareness.

The magic here is your personal awareness. This is where you realize something in the consciousness. This is the ability to filter through all of the messages you are bombarded with minute to minute from many sources and directions. Finding and focusing an awareness of surroundings, and particular issues that only per-tain to YOU. That is having the power of awareness and forgiving the guilt we feel. To say to ourselves it is okay to say no to the issues and drama that are not in alignment with our life's journey.

Knowing your Strength and Setting Limits

Each and every day we are given the opportunity to help and do things for family, friends, coworkers and community. We can manage to be strong for other people, but while helping others we may feel unable to set stable healthy boundaries. Oftentimes this results in us extending our help too far. This creates prob-lems and may make us vulnerable and wronged in the end. We must forgive ourselves for giving too much to others. We must set limits, and respect our own feelings despite what others may think or believe. The most bold thing to do is admit I can't be everywhere for everyone. We have the privilege to say no and be adamant about it too. Boundaries are imperative, and it's okay to have a personal value of limits for health reasons alone. Too often we aren't courageous to say no and are encouraged to set aside our value systems for others. We must recognize our strength and learn to be firm with our limits.

Firm limits are a crucial self-check for anyone working on moving forward to forgiveness. Knowing what you are capable of is the touchstone of setting limits for others. Your needs, abil-ities and capacity are what need to be measured when setting limits. Other people's expectations, requirements or judgment should not even be considered if it means we end up agreeing to something we cannot complete or going against our beliefs to follow through. We cannot forgive if we are still bowing to pressure and being manipulated into stepping over our boundaries. When limits are fully in place, we are mentally ready to move forward in healing.

Speak Softly and Know the Truth

There have been too many times when we have watched people say the wrong things at the wrong time because they wanted to control the situation. Other times we personally wanted to say something, but we couldn't. Our lack of judgment due to fear, worry or control causes us to freeze when the time comes to speak up. Other times our better judgement comes too late because we react without thinking it through. Prior to these situations, and afterward, it is a good idea if we analyze why we back down and keep our thoughts and beliefs to ourselves. Are we afraid to show our inner most side to others because of what they might think or would say?

No one ever enjoys being vulnerable to criticism. We have all been judged by words and we can all probably agree it wasn't pleasant feeling. Today we must accept the responsibility to tell the truth, and not sacrifice our own life for someone else because of fear or being afraid of judgment. We can always be empathetic, but the core here is we must be truthful about our feelings and that takes much courage. Thinking things through and speaking with poise, thought and accuracy can ensure the truth of what we speak is conveyed with proper intention.

(NIV, Gen 3:15)

Reckless words pierce like a sword, but the tongue of the wise brings healing.

Proverbs 12:18

It is always a smart idea to wait and question thy self about the emotion one is feeling before blurting it out. Such resentment, anger, excitement or opinion may not be well taken or might not reflect out true beliefs and values. Often out initial emotional response overrides our true intentions. Finding patience and forgiveness for yourself and others will bring a better mental aptitude and a warmer feeling of self-control. Holding your tongue during emotional or upsetting interactions is a skill that requires practice and determination. Otherwise, emotion easily boils, overtaking any intention to speak softly. During emotional outbursts, truth is mangled into words filled with negative emotion.

Knowing We are Not the Target

Too many times we allow others to put unnecessary blame on our decisions and feelings. We need to forgive these people and forgive ourselves for falling into the convoluted idea that they have any power over us. Moving forward we have learned what we require and realized that some people's intentions do not have our best interests at heart. Quite the contrary, people can seek to try to decide what we should do and influence our thinking for reasons that have nothing to do with us.

Many people are unhappy with their own lives and they project their pain onto you and your life. Rather than calling and speaking to you directly, out of authentic concern they make up stuff just to make themselves look good. We must also forgive their naïve judgment. and have the courage to turn the cheek and say it's okay that we don't agree and don't care, because only I know the truth what's best for me. ❖

PERSONAL AFFAIRS
ॐ

Friends and Family

Friends and family are capable of causing unforgivable injuries that can destroy our lives as we know them and cause damage that feels irreparable. Friendships, like other intimate relationships, are sustained through presumed implicit trust. In strong friendships as in marriages, people extend their hearts and possessions to each other, share each other's secrets and trust no one will use the friendship or relationship for her own advantage or to cause intentional harm to the other. The injury can be mild or severe, from a physical injury to the reputation in the local community. The usual experience is petty gossip, back stabbing and hypocrisy over jealousy or misunderstanding. We have relationships with special sets of expectations some stated, some implies. Some of our relationships are purer than marital relationships in the intimacy, honesty and collaboration that occur. We choose who we allow as friends, business partners and acquaintances too. Friends have influence on our personal choices we make, which can be beneficial or detrimental depending on whose interests they have at heart.

Enduring friends are those who are in our lives and provide constant support whenever it is needed. These friends are essential in helping people think thru their decisions they make and get back on course when confusion or the conflict is affecting one's life. The moral part of history between good friends may include being honest, providing mutual support, retaining secrets and above all not harming the friendship or the other person. A special kind of trust must be in place and there is a balance involved. When family members or friends fail to support one another, the wounds can be deep and long lasting. They can damage the concept of pure trust itself by causing the person to question everything and everyone in their lives. When a trusted friend breaks the relationship through malicious actions, it can be difficult to open ourselves up to opportunities for new people in our lives. An unforgivable lie can signal that nowhere is there anyone we simply can trust. It goes to the core of the person who's been betrayed, hardening the heart against future hurt.

As much hurt anyone can bring you, competing emotions hurt further by allowing it to expand and envelop us. Many sleepless nights can be tormented by hatred and aggravated through seemingly endless days obscured by exhaustion. Dwelling in this place for any length of time can bring you to the brink of collapse. Hatred is an emotion most of us feel uncomfortable with. Sometimes it is something to suffer thru rather than soak in the negativity and a wounded person is stronger for it. We are told not to hate from early on in our lives. When people who are able to forgive, come through the other side of betrayal, they come to admit the depth of their hatred.

* * *

This anger and hurt is compounded when a long-term relationship, often with a family member, is negative, derogatory or abusive. Feelings of guilt and personal failure are compounded when someone who claims to love us, hurts us repeatedly. Over many years we try to incite change in their behavior so they will alter their interactions. It is as though we know they love us so they must want to change themselves so they do not lose us. In reality many people do not change because they cannot or will not confront the fear holding them back. There are people in my life and I always thought they would change, but they didn't.

Unfortunately it is our family and close friends who are capable of hurting us the most. Not only do we often trust them with our heart and soul, they are the first people we contact with secrets and uncertainties. They are also the people we feel the most lost without, people we rely on for support in all aspects of our lives.

Divorce and Broken Relationships

Personal and close relationships that end abruptly don't have to be filled with feelings of anger or loss. These surprise endings can be seen as a gift and a chance to grow emotionally, physically or spiritually. Looking at the greater picture and life's purpose, even if we are not experiencing great joy, can be a place to start. Faith plays a big role in realizing that everything is set in place for a reason specific to our journey. An abrupt, upsetting loss of a relationship can truly be a blessing in disguise.

As a co-partner of the relationship, we must accept the good with the bad. Choosing this attitude or mindset will allow you to move forward more quickly. It also removes you from being a victim. Forgiveness is a powerful release, but it takes time to evaluate the right perspective and you must be ready and able to change your life around. Relinquishing old pain, insults and anger will free your mind, heart and spirit to a life that awaits you. Below are a list of things we can forgive our partners, friendships, business and other relationships and ourselves from intentionally causing hurt:

- Insults, harsh words and derogatory comments
- Physical and emotional abuse
- Not being physically or emotionally available
- Anger expressed inappropriately
- Infidelity whether, spoken, physical or implied
- Blame and guilt
- Judgment of actions, words or behaviors
- Choosing a dysfunctional partner
- Choosing to stay with a dysfunctional partner
- Not loving self enough to be a functional partner
- Enabling out of fear, uncertainty or worry
- Believing you must settle in relationship
- Feeling isolated or alone
- Alcohol and drug use and abuse
- Toxic language and responses
- Using the children against the other parent and other children
- Gossip to family and community
- Feelings of insecurity
- Expectations of how a person will act or behave
- Not interested or available as a support person when needed
- Believe life will get better with time without inner change
- Making excuses and not trying to change ✤

TREATMENT

How many times have you ever thought you were not worthy of success, happiness, or supportive and loving relationships? Listen, when we believe we aren't worthy of being treated well, we will accept nothing less and most importantly life will not progress in a forward motion. Innately, we deserve positive relationships and interactions but that does not always happen. Our challenge is to be good to ourselves, treating ourselves and others as we want others to treat us.

One should never do wrong in return, nor mistreat any man, no matter how one has been mistreated by him.

Socrates

People will disappoint us and cause us harm if we give them power over our potential. When this occurs, fast thoughts often fly to revenge or harboring ill feelings towards that person. Unfortunately that only serves to extend the negativity and allows the ill will to continue. There is too much else to do, so don't limit your endless possibilities of great life. Give yourself the gift of forgiveness and you no longer are the person you were. Start living today! ✤

ABILITY TO FORGIVE

Foregiveness of Self

The key to releasing guilt is to recognize that we all go through life doing the very best we can with the limited skills and awareness that we have at the time. Unfortunately, the awareness that we have is seldom enough. As a result, we make mistakes. Sometimes big ones that seem insurmountable at the time, especially when they are initiated with well thought out intentions, things do not always go the way we intend them to. Making mistakes is just part of the human process, a fact of life. That's how we learn. Every time you make a mistake, you learn a little more about life. You become a little wiser and a little more aware. In this way mistakes are blessings as they lead us away from the non-beneficial which open us to opportunities of pure bliss and fulfillment.

If you look, the most valuable lessons you have ever learned are lessons that you could only have learned the hard way. It's too bad that we have to learn so much by making mistakes. The real tragedy happens when we add guilt. The moment you add guilt, you seriously damage your relationship with yourself. You lose your confidence and your self-respect. You reinforce the feelings of not being okay. You feel undeserving and you hold yourself back. Guilt seems to be caused by what you did, but it's not guilt by the mistake that was made. Guilt is something you add later with benefit and hindsight. It was only after you discovered the consequences of your actions that you add guilt.

The moment you made your mistake, you were doing exactly what you thought you should, and given the state of mind you were in at the time. Only with hindsight could you have acted differently. Even though you knew better, your level of knowing wasn't enough to change your actions. You certainly didn't know the consequences as well as you do today. But we should have known, no nonsense, our internal conflict is hard on ourselves. You couldn't have known one moment before you did. Making the mistake is how you learned.

(NIV, Gen 3:15)
Brothers and sisters, I know that I still have a long way to go. But there is one thing I do: I forget what is in the past and try as hard as I can to reach the goal before me.

Philippians 3:13

Five years from now you're going to be wiser than you are today, but the wisdom you're going to have in five years doesn't do any of us good today. Living in the present, you only know what you know today. Likewise the wisdom that you have today didn't do you any good back then, you only knew what you knew. So forgive your not knowing. Are you willing to forgive yourself for not being wiser? Do you believe you did the very best you could, given what you knew at the time? Maybe now you suffered enough. Are you willing to be free of guilt? Have you punished yourself enough? See if you're willing to set yourself free. Or do so, bit by bit, every day.

Forgiveness and Kindness

Society is brutal, on our self-esteem. As we have watched, maybe even played into as a victim, it appears society says yes, it's acceptable to disgrace a person. It's permissible to make someone feel inferior, force someone through shame, or make available the capacity to make someone feel unworthy. In fact society, through the media and elsewhere, encourages division and competition which results in harmful beliefs about shaming and making derogatory comments. There is nothing beneficial about this societal belief and it causes negative self-worth and reliance on acceptance so unique individuals feel unwelcome. Kindness goes hand in hand with forgiveness, as virtues of positive souls to see an integrated human existence rather than one divided with conflict.

The complexities are more salient when kindness is compared to our current societal norms. How about when someone asks to be pardoned or exonerated, why is it socially or culturally prohibited, offensive, or unacceptable? We all know that to ask for forgiveness is fundamentally crucial, as it's needed for a life full of knowing and zest. Disregarding society and the many complexities and disputes, it's nobler to take the higher road and offer forgiveness. It seems, however, more popular to brand criminals with their mistakes for life, refuse to move past someone's transgression and focus on constantly reminding them of what they have down wrong. Since we cannot alter society immediately, we must affect change by being the change we want to see and emulate an attitude of kindness and forgiveness.

If we do not take the time to forgive ourselves there's a chance of something going wrong. If it can be avoided, no one ever wants to invite bad consequence. That being said, it is time to practice forgiveness for ourselves and others to strengthen our focus on the future and moving toward a better life. Choosing to be kind to ourselves requires daily practice and devotion.

These are the few ways we can practice humility:
To speak as little as possible of one's self.
To mind one's own business.
Not to want to manage other people's affairs.
To avoid curiosity.
To accept contradictions and correction cheerfully.
To pass over the mistakes of others.
To accept insults and injuries.
To accept being slighted, forgotten and disliked.
To be kind and gentle even under provocation.
Never to stand on one's dignity.
To choose always the hardest.
~ Mother Teresa, The Joy in Loving:
A Guide to Daily Living

Our time should be devoted to general well-being and that is to let go and move on of all negativity blocking progress. Choose to pass mercy to those who have hurt you and find the ability to behave kindly even to ourselves with forgiveness. Believing love is the answer and striving to let go of hurt feelings and misunderstanding is a path that requires kindness before forgiveness is even possible.

Forgiveness and Power

There are many people who allow anger to have power over them. They fixate on what they perceive to be the problem and focus anger and negativity on that person or situation. Anger can become an eternal cycle, eating away at potential and stealing their power. Also, anger is a draining emotion, pulling energy and effort away from your true goal. If someone is perpetually angry it makes it difficult to show forgiveness and trying to do so can become an annoyance.

In order to forgive we must not let anyone have reasoning power over us or over our emotions and reactions to relationships and circumstances. We have the right to our opinion and the right to respond in the emotionally correct way that is suitable for us as an individual. We don't have to be in agreement, as we certainly could agree to disagree. Forgiveness is not about giving power to a person or ideology. On the contrary, it is taking back power and not allowing the unforgivable to affect our lives or hold us back for one second longer. If we position ourselves with a better way of thinking, our concentration can be majority focused on our own forgiveness and power within.

Choosing Forgiveness

When we say I forgive myself or I'm sad and I regret what happened, but I forgive myself because I choose to; it is an act of releasing yourself from guilt. With time and repetition, this is particularly easy. It's when you are tired of feeling worthless or not being good enough, finding out what your actions say about you, and feeling the hurt enough to move forward. Allowing yourself to feel human is a choice you have to make for yourself. You have to choose forgiveness every time if you want the benefits it provides.

What is needed to be free of guilt? Forgiveness for everything you have done. Know that you always did the very best that you could do with the limited skills and awareness available at the time. You love yourself enough to understand that everything that happened before now was in the past and not worth beating yourself up about. The guilt is a lack of faith or a disappointment caused by out-of-character actions. Forgiving is an act of faith, knowledge that there is potential to be guilt-free in love, through God. Now surrender to that knowledge and be comforted.

(NIV, Gen 3:15)
Let love and faithfulness never leave you.

Proverbs 2:3

Not only is forgiveness a choice but it has to be made over and over again in faith that love is the better way, the way to the life you dream of. Every time we doubt, anger and upset creeps in about past issues or experiences; hurt caused by self or others. Doubt is an opportunity to confirm your belief in a better way. Obliterating doubt with faith is the path to the better way. Once you have chosen to have faith, to forgive every hurtful action you see and experience, you are living life on your terms because you are choosing to forgive the unforgivable.

Life opposes many daily difficulties; just how many do you want? You have the opportunity to add or subtract difficulties through forgiveness. Choosing to be mindful of our own goals and acts of forgiveness provides personal positivity and reduces difficulties. We will not make everyone happy, so you need to make note of that and start making plans for your happiness starting today. You are only responsible for your own happiness so forgive the ignorance of others and choose the life you are here for.

The purpose of forgiveness is to progress and recover from whatever is holding you back in your life. Depending on the circumstances the capacity of forgiveness can be very dreadful and daunting. Meaning the very thought of forgiving the unforgivable is emotionally and physically overpowering. Getting over a bad break up, fight, death, job loss, or finished friendship is never, ever enjoyable. However, with a slice of faith, forgiving ourselves can reduce and soften the discomfort. The challenge to forgive shouldn't be such a nuisance because we have already made peace with it in our own hearts. The troublesome agony that somebody or something has disappeared should not cause us to wallow in guilt or self-depreciation because we have taken actions to move forward, to let go and not allow the unforgivable to define our lives any longer.

The progression of forgiveness varies from one person to another and it's imperative not to rush unless you are ready to forgive. But without it you will be treading water in the shallow end of the pool. It isn't until you realize you have the courage and understanding about self and esteem that you will realize you can stand up and won't drown. Time to forgive the intolerable is now. Doing so requires many conscious acts of forgiveness derived from a strong belief within.

Forgiving the Intolerable

When is the right time to release yourself physically from toxic obligation? Probably the first day you feel an unpleasant sensation, and your intuition says absolutely not or no more. Those feelings may include experiencing difficulties, being upset or even impaired by collateral damage. As soon as the thoughts and accompanying emotions begin to play out, involving any intolerable incident, practice letting go of these limiting negativities. In the long term, you will know yourself better through forgiveness and will not allow anything to impact your life in such a negative way ever again.

Depending on your personal experiences, you may be working on forgiving something horrific. When severe trauma is experienced, the soft still moments of healing come slowly. Putting aside expectations on yourself or your family, if they are making this journey with you, provides you with a clean slate to start moving forward out of the darkness. There is not a specific time period on forgiveness. There is no cut and dry period between happiness and despair. It is a process that begins with a spark. The spark can be faith, hope, wanting more for yourself, the gleam in your child's eye or anything small that you can grasp, that enables you to see a light guiding you out of the hurt. No matter how bad it gets hold on to that spark and build faith, build hope and build your life towards happiness.

Coming to terms with your life and experiences and social tolerances is actually a positive response to making a transformation. This is when you make a substitution for variables, transforming the family cycle and modification within your brain. Leading yourself into a happier way and altering behavior to promote self-health is a way to make a permanent change to positivity. No longer complying to give into something tempting, harmful or expected because of past choices and transgressions. No more struggles to counterattack, but to say no, because you dared to put a protective coating around your heart. You have practiced forgiveness and you are eager to let go, for your own good. Ceasing the negative, nurturing the passion and keeping this feeling, or thought of what drives you, alive so you may have a beautiful life.

Why Must We Forgive?

Forgiveness is a personal choice, free will to let go. Christians are taught to forgive just as Jesus forgave his persecutors and so too will we be forgiven for what we do to self and others. Don't think that this has been a walk in the park for me or others who have experienced betrayal, because it isn't. It can be extremely hard to let anything go if you don't have a solid rhyme, reason or comprehension of why it happened in the first place. Until we have answers to why and how things happened and what the person was feeling, it can be difficult to move on. If something is inconceivable to us, we dwell on it. We fight the feelings, but really what are we fighting? It already happened, move on right? But the emotional human beast inside says I want to go against the grain, because I'm stubborn; I was hurt so now I must dwell in the hurt. This is a harmful cycle that does nothing but keep us miserable. Forgiveness stops the cycle and provides a chance to increase love through prayer.

(NIV, Gen 3:15)
But I say to you, love your enemies and pray for those who persecute you.
Matthew 5:44

In reality our faith and understanding says God is in charge of everything and we must let him toil with what needs to be solved. Regardless we can facilitate somethings, but ultimately it's the heavenly father's plan. We are just the messengers and must strive to move forward with love. Go beyond what happened, who hurt us or how mistakes were made and give those emotions to God with unrestrained forgiveness.

Meaning of Forgiveness

Forgiveness is a word that has been tossed around loosely for years. What does it exactly mean anyway? The word itself means to stop feeling angry towards someone or something. Commonly it is understood that forgiveness comes when someone admits they have done wrong and are sorry. People ask for forgiveness when they have done someone wrong either intentionally or not. In this context all of the power is in the hands of the one causing harm or hurt. This is not the case. True forgiveness comes from within and happens regardless of other people's intentions. It is a personal intention to live life based on loving kindness and mutual respect. This personal intention involves forgiving or letting go of the powerful hold a person or situation has over the feelings and emotions of another. Forgiving is freedom and is resting within each of us.

When we say forgive, it means letting go of all arguments and inhibitions we feel. The sensation of freedom from a burden is actually a chance to be at peace. Of course our will, desires and expectations have everything to do with that too. It's important to remember God respects our commitment to honor and to praise him when we find true forgiveness from the heart. Forgiveness truthfully is about pardoning, that's how we learned, and we actually forgave. Great freedom comes within.

Patience and Forgiveness

Forgiveness takes a great deal of practice and patience. We all have had so many days and nights feeling hurt and forlorn and the pain was too intolerable to be repaired. Ever find yourself so steaming mad and wanted answers and accountability, because someone unjustly hurt you? Ever just grow tired of people hurting you, and the need to know how to protect yourself from being wounded again? It is easy to become distrustful, harbor anger and hurt feelings and isolate ourselves. It is much more difficult to accept and embrace forgiveness happening through small steps of patient faith.

If you want to make things right, you will want to cover all ends and to heal correctly without any relapses. Who needs the remembrance of a broken heart? It's liberating when you are free and no longer bound by guilt or anger. Imagine the possibilities. That is my beauty secret, and the true power of forgiveness. Let go of any illusions that this process is a quickie. It is slow and it will continue as long as you want it to. It is a process that requires patience. Letting go of the past is promising but the time-consuming nature of letting go can be daunting. I mean from personal experience, I couldn't change my circumstances for my family or the people around me overnight. However, patiently allowing forgiveness opened my heart and allowed me a chance to develop and produce instinctive qualities about forgiveness.

Difference Between Letting Go and Forgetting

First of all they are not the same thing. Forgiving people takes honor and power that take serious reflection and time to process, understand, accept and have faith in. Letting go takes a course all by itself. Forgiving is a choice made consciously to disallow the hurt to continue. Letting go is a process that happens more easily once the choice to forgive has been made. It's much easier as the issues become more faint and your past becomes less of an issue. The Lord works very hard developing our inner strength and will to conquer anything. Be patient with yourself and let the process occur while retaining the lessons learned.

Forgetting, on the other hand, implies it could happen again. Quite the contrary, when forgiveness of self occurs, there is no place for forgetting the harm people or situations can cause. Inner strength, faith and love are built up so that instead of forgetting and perchance to encounter it again, we have built a wall of protection around ourselves to protect from the potential of forgetting. Like scars from a wound, letting go through forgiveness is a healing process but there will always be marks left behind to remind us we are stronger for what happened.

Forgive and forget is a common phrase but it should be forgive and move forward in knowledge. To forget is to open yourself up to the same negativity or hurt through a new relationship or situation. Letting go, or forgiving is an exercise in self-worth and self-improvement separate from the person, incident or mistake you are forgiving. It is a process through which our inner selves are asking to for us to be patient.

Signs of Unwillingness to Forgive

Forgiveness is a process one must be willing to go through. Not opening yourself up to forgiveness prohibits the healing process to continue and prevents forward motion in the direction of a better life. If you are still stuck on one or more of the following misconceptions regarding forgiveness you might not be ready to move on. If you find this to be the case, work through it slowly, always acknowledging the validity of your feelings and striving for the betterment of your situation.

1. Forgiveness requires something of the other person first.
   * They have to say sorry.
   * We must make them see they are wrong.
2. This wrongdoing and resentment has become part of my identity.
   * Openly sharing the hurt or betrayal with everyone brings pleasure.
   * Make sure everyone knows my side of the story and ensure they feel angry also.
3. What are the pleasures of this anger and resentment?
   * Is there something to be gained from the conflict?
   * Holding on to the anger, not ready to let go.
4. Is there a part of me that wants to entertain the anger?
   * Feeling justified by intolerable actions.
   * Anger allows us to revel in the wrongdoing.
5. Is withholding forgiveness about my ego?
   * Judging the behavior as not deserving forgiveness.
   * Not wanting to be perceived as a hypocrite or quitter.
6. What would forgiveness look like?

- Where do you start to forgive the unforgivable?
- Breaking the cycle seems overwhelming.
7. Is this where I want to stay?
   - Want better for yourself.
   - Allow possibility rather than stay stuck.

Why We Have Resentments

Whenever we have been deeply hurt by someone we once cared for, it's understandable why we become unhappy, inflamed and jumbled. It's usually due to love. When our feelings are permitted to delay and reminisce on the past, something happens to our self-esteem and resentment takes over in our mind and heart. The pain is abundant and at times it can make you feel powerless if you don't get ahold of why you're so gloomy. Rather than getting so engulfed in what is amiss, try not cheating yourself from your future. Holding that resentment will make anyone depressed and lose self-worth and a physical link with others in your life that are worthy of your time. As you continue to release yourself from the resentment, you will experience empathy and consideration, because you no longer hold onto the heartache that brought you here.

Even if our resentment is justified and we are still appalled by the heinous treatment we received, we must love ourselves enough to let it go. The resentment we feel is a sign that something that happen is not in align with our values and beliefs. This is all the more reason to move forward so that we can once again focus on a positive plan for the future. Resentment on its own will simply drag you down into despair no longer moving towards goals or living in faith and love.

When You Can't Forgive Someone

Forgiveness certainly can have its challenges particularly if the person who hurt you never confesses their wrongdoing or never offers a possibility that they are sorry. Sometimes a person can blatantly hurt you without consideration or care. Forgiveness is a process for everyone no matter the size of pain. We will continue to revisit the things that bring sadness over and over again until we get it right or until we stop the discomfort and that comes with time and experience.

> *Forgiveness has nothing to do with absolving a criminal of his crime. It has everything to do with relieving oneself of the burden of being a victim--letting go of the pain and transforming oneself from victim to survivor.*
>
> C.R. Strahan

The insistence on making people pay for their transgressions, in our society, sometimes forces people to look a little more closely at the reality of what they insist. Each movement forward provides a small lesson in letting go of the pain.

In order to forgive, it's important to remember forgiveness is our responsibility to ourselves. Such loyalty commands respect, as it requires us to be different so life can transform. It's very important to distance ourselves from being a victim and taking back all control and power from the person who held you back. Letting go of resentment, will empower you to have consideration and sympathy. This takes strength of personal fortitude and of faith to work slowly at being able to come to forgiveness.

Forget the Anger and Resentments

Name the particular wound.

Name the spark that hurts the most.

Name the person whom offended you.

Let it go, let it go, LET IT GO!

Self-Reflect YOU ARE LOVED AND YOU ARE VALUABLE

Do this every day until forgiveness is attainable. Once you have done it for all anger (for about a month) you will always find something luscious.

Compassion and Forgiveness

You cannot be compassionate when you're sitting in judgment of the person! Forgiveness is a must. Maybe through understanding of life we have humility. We no longer have the desire to put ourselves ahead of others to make us feel good. When we've fully understood this, we treat everyone with quality and respect. When we have compassion there are no rules of judgment.

> (NIV, Gen 3:15)
> *Judge not, and you will not be judged; condemn not and you will not be condemned; forgive and you will be forgiven.*
>
> Luke 6:37

Forgiveness allows us to work towards true compassion and love. Through forgiveness we come to understand humanity and we can see ourselves reflected in the actions of others. Having compassion for the person, not the action, eventually seems to encourage more love.

Why We Forgive

When we forgive, we simply feel better. We eliminate the pain of past suffering. After that our hearts are open to love. Forgiveness is to be taken seriously, because it's truly a gift to us. When it's time to let go and look to forgiveness as an alternative you might experience some of the following:

- Highly critical accusatory or making demands with others & self.
- Turmoil over the past is affecting the present.
- Feeling panicked or anxious and alone.
- Enduring pain, mental anguish and feeling needy.
- Regretting or having harsh feelings about something or someone.
- Always pushing to be right.
- Self-sabotaging positive aspects or relationships.
- Choices based on what we believe will makes up happy, but don't because we rushed without thinking, now there is nervous apprehension.
- Intuition about needing to move forward in life.
- Judgment acceptance from others.
- Our thoughts develop opinions of the way the world should be. If we go through life wondering what's wrong with someone else or what is wrong with ourselves we are teaching our mind and our vision to only see imperfections. Simply stating it does not work and there is a problem. Judgments are not short little conversations. We're putting this information into our consciousness, and by doing so these actions called judgments will divide and isolate us.

Bottom line judging is powerless and very disrespectful. For your minds, stop judging others and see the possibilities of each moment.

- To surrender any or all of your personal power is using one's intuition to personal choice. It is not filled with someone else's guidelines and judgment. Surrender is not the opinion of another. It's one person's personal choice to make a decision.

Mother and Forgiveness

As parents no one was given a book on the code of ethics of how to be the best parent ever. Most parents fly by the seat of their pants and hope everything works out well. Sometimes it does, and sometimes it does not. Usually if there's conflict all parties are hurt in the end because of actions or things said. Whatever the origin of pain it's imperative that you understand what made the individual feel so angry and why so much emotion was placed on blame. This attempt at understanding is a step towards forgiveness. It's all too convenient to point the finger and bring misguided shame and justification to the wrong party. It seems childish one party can run their mouth and act as if they had no part in any of it. That's disrespectful. And on top admit no responsibility for wrongdoing? Showing no guilt only to cause unnecessary guilt. Whether the issue lies with the parents or the child there should be a request for forgiveness. It's all too easy to be relaxed and informal as this is not a difficult situation from the one party pointing the finger. It takes great courage and healthy mind to start the healing by forgiving the mother or father, son or daughter we were. Knowing helps others understand so we can become better than we were rather than dwell in rumors or with the unknown. It's also important to comprehend what reasons and purposes you need to forget so to nurture and safeguard forgiveness.

(NIV, Gen 3:15)
Father, forgive them, for they know not what they do.
Luke 34:34

By remembering, when our children are young, that they need guidance and forgiveness we will allow them to learn to forgive others. It can be difficult in a position of power to seek forgiveness of our children for our past transgressions whether they were intentional or not. As children are growing and learning they will cause hurt, choose harmful or intolerable actions. As Jesus asked forgiveness of the people who crucified them for not having the knowledge or faith to know what they were doing wrong. So to we need to forgive our children for the hurt they cause as they are growing, learning and developing. This is an opportunity to bring forgiveness full circle and instill in the next generation the importance of forgiveness.

Offering Forgiveness

When acknowledging the truth, one must determine what exactly they may have done to offend someone else. The challenge here, is calculating the wrongdoings of ourselves without judging, because after all we're only human and there is room for error. When we are deeply sorry for any wrongdoing we must not only follow through with regrets and sorrow, but we must also ask to be forgiven without defenses. This is never easy because we can't force our opinions on others especially having anyone forgive you. No one can release you from that obligation as we are on their time and that includes understandings another's feelings and their ability to believe you.

Look back in forgiveness, forward in hope, down in compassion, and up with gratitude.

— Zig Zigler

Benefits of Forgiveness

Releasing resentments and unpleasantness can provide positive change to personal health, happiness, and freedom. Many wonderful benefits of forgiveness can be:

- Mental calmness
- Less hypertension
- Improved self-respect
- Suggestive good health
- Restored connections
- Psychologically sound
- Stress reduction
- Focus on what matters ✧

PEACE

Compassionate to Ourselves

Why is it so hard to open our life to others, especially our heart? Is it because we are afraid to be vulnerable? As a rule in any new relationship whether, personal, love or working relationship, we are extremely susceptible physically, psychologically weak and open to all kinds of attacks and liable to misery. Often we feel a need to fit in or are eager to please or feel accepted. It can be easy to be pressured in the moment. So it is only natural to be exposed and, feeling helpless, to fear. The ability to see the light at the end of the tunnel is also the disposition to do whatever it takes to do the right thing, despite being difficult or even incomprehensible. Something done with a loving heart out wins any rejection.

When we act with compassion to ourselves we are remembering past hurt and helping ourselves move to forgiveness. The act of compassion on our individual selves is one that brings peace as it encourages an alignment of beliefs to faith. This enables us to live simply in our quest for a life full of authenticity.

Equanimity

Emotional control is something we all need for forgiveness. When we don't have it we struggle personally. Reorganizing your thoughts and schedule so you're not exhausted and over programmed, is one way to regain control. Lately society is filled with toxins of all kinds and promotions encouraging you to take more to keep going. When is it enough to say no more devotion to drug dependence, caffeine and unhealthy addictions, no more being pre-occupied with the physical side of life. Taking a different course of action requires promised devotion, complete surrender. Anything is possible, even a calm and untroubled life without clouds.

> (NIV, Gen 3:15)
> *Whoever is forgiven much, loves much.*
> Luke 7:47

In order to obtain this we must forgive ourselves enough to enter peace, quiet time in our hearts, mind and body. This act of giving is something easily gained if we are willing to break old habits with new ones called tranquility. Faith is something more powerful than you; however that resonates with you, is essential to move towards love.

Tranquility

Tranquility is a discipline that is free from commotion. All one needs is a significant mental calmness in a peaceful location free from noise. Undisturbed moments filled with private silence where you can hear your inner voice speak to you crystal clear are crucial. This type of peace takes abundant forgiveness of self and courage to understand the true meaning of untouched stillness, so that you may hear your inner most serene thoughts.

Something as subtle and delicate as the notion of tranquility permits our inner guidance to give us a keen sense of direction amid the calm. This is the acceptance of the truth of solitude-filled peace and gives rise in our ability to trust in our intuition. The tranquility of understanding is what you call awareness to be forgiven.

Comforting Words

Our thoughts are acquired knowledge and to be in control of our minds is one of the most problematic and aggravating jobs we ever partake in. With control comes the possibility of a peaceful mind and comforting words. Calmly expressing forgiveness and pursuit of happiness through a life of love, these words bring relief and security.

When is the right moment to measure those intervals? Afraid of the time or courage it will take to make those alterations?
If you accept something as truthful and genuine, only then you can believe it can exist. You are in charge of your emotion, your ideas and the direction of your pathway is no one else's decision. All your preparation needs to be lived out articulated with expression of care. First have the power to forgive thy self and anyone that has ever hurt you. This will be a forever process and we have no choice but to manage our personal affairs. Sometimes it's in the experience that we accidentally discover, and in misery we make a verdict, because we have had enough sadness. We are finally conscious of our own condition allowing us to make decisions about our life and what we will no longer

accept. Without admission and a dose of humility, we will not reach our goal. Understanding what a meaningful unit of language can bring will result in positive feeling and emotion to your life. Being as good as your word is the difference of opinion when you are confronting comforting words. Being brief and concisely expressed with powerful choices will be your promise to electing what is good from what is unnecessary or a waste of time. Starting your thoughts with I have, I want, I will and I trust is essential. ✣

COMPREHENSION

Life's Credit

There are many demands today with work, family and bills that are putting added pressures on our time. Personal energy is dissipating and can leave you feeling emotionally drained and physically wasted. When you are balanced, your life is strong. How does that happen? If you treat your life like a blank checking account, with daily deposits and withdrawals, make sure you are making deposits and withdrawals to the personal account of YOU...this includes emotional state such as feelings, frame of mind, and inner spirit.

This is not a joke as too often we make many withdrawals and deplete any energy left in that personal account and the debt continues to grow. Sadly enough we permit others close to us to make those withdrawals for us. We need less debt and more credit. Being overdrawn absolutely can ruin your life. No one ever wants to be in the red; sad and depressed.

The goal in life is to build credit, not be overdrawn. This means being responsible with our life, letting go of drama and going after the life we deserve. This requires much attention to the life you want to have. If you want the best, it's time to face the music and let go of whatever holds you back. Find the forgiveness to let it all go, so you can build on that personal account.

The Quality of Love

Loving is the tender affection you have for someone regardless of outside influence; feelings of goodwill toward an individual. Either you have it or you don't. It's the desire for someone or something you want very much. Maybe it's to show the act of kindness to someone through strong affection. It's also called a romantic affair, a beloved. I'm sure we all acknowledge the unpleasant or ill-mannered situation where a relationship goes amiss. It is imperative to recognize and have courage to admit the past, as it shows awareness and understanding of hurt or loss. Take the time necessary to address all concerns of past relationships and calmly leave it in the past in order to move onward. Rather than delve into a new relationship, the emotional distress and any feelings of discomfort need to be dealt with. Only then, relaxed and informed, you will be able to take on any new romances because you did not rush, and were capable of letting go with complete forgiveness. To love one must be available, meaning unattached, eligible and accessible to mind, body and spirit.

It is impossible to love others if you don't love yourself. The sad truth is often we do not realize we do not love ourselves until we are buried in a situation that is much bigger than us. This is why it is so important to do a self-check. Make sure you are treating yourself with love. How do you love yourself or how do you know if you love yourself? These questions themselves show a concern for the individual. Concern for self, belies love of self. And forgiveness can be a huge potential in promoting self-love.

Gratification

A sense of wellbeing is very important, just how do we obtain it? A noteworthy study concludes the immune system responds adamantly when we help another person. That doesn't mean it is advisable to help everyone in your path and get burned. What it means is have the nerve to get strong and care for you first. Out of that comes natural abundant love to help others without anything in return. It also means helping others, helps us. We are all connected and rely on mutual love and assistance for a comfortable existence.

Once we know what we desire in life, no matter how big or small, we have to choose actions to move forward and achieve these goals. Making small goals can be an easy way to see progress and feel gratified.

Receiving from Another

It's never easy to admit to others you need help. But it's a known fact that allowing others to help you is healthy. When we are valuable and beneficial to others, we often neglect the gift we have come to receive instead of asking for help or graciously accepting it.

Regardless of break up or a great loss, a clear sign to ask for direction from others is when one is miserable, down or sick. Inquiring for help is needed more than ever, despite how terrifying it is to ask someone. The question that remains is which person is most qualified to help? Is it a family member, friend or stranger? That's something you will have to question or ponder, as you are the one whom is capable of making that final decision. And it may depend on the situation or reason help is needed. Different people can provide empathy, distraction or something else depending on the situation.

It's much easier for us to move past the isolated belief that we don't need anyone or we can handle everything all on our own. Making allowances for imperfection is never easy. Be merciful for what you don't know, and give yourself a pardon of forgiveness. Life wasn't meant to be lived alone. Reach for the things we require and long for in life and go get them, especially if they seem reasonable. No need to justify your life to anyone, ever.

Eliminating Should, Have To and Can't

We know inspiration gives us the ability to be creative and motivated. Having said that what holds that encouragement or reassurance that all will be fair? Absolutely nothing. It's part of the game of life. Nothing ventured, nothing gained. Sometimes we are motivated by confident people, who are hopeful. Other times we are turned off by negative bashers who have an opinion, but don't have a clue to what you're talking about. Those people are all around us, they may be our closest friends or family or our own inner voice, hurt by past trauma. They tell us you can't and you have to…do you ever wonder how to disregard this negative opinion? It's all in words. Each one has an argument or a difference of opinion. You have to decide which words work for you and which ones you will not accept. At least not only listening to how they work but the way you talk too.

The words themselves dictate a response by communicating a forceful demand. "have to" and "can't" are words of absolutes. There is no bending or accepting real world reasons or understandings. "Should" is a word that brings connotations of guilt by explaining how things ought to go in the future. The negative and dictatorial aspect of the words is not conducive to forgiveness or moving forward.

Removing the assurance that we should, have to, or can't do something frees us to be who we are. These assumptions most often come from external sources and have zero validity. Seeing these words as limitations and thereby removing them is beneficial for self-improvement.

Reprogramming our minds to think and speak differently takes a lot of work. It takes compassion, understanding and discipline. Being conscious ensures you have calm and controlled behavior. Having order and the capacity to do something also means controlling influence on your life, which will give you great strength and the authority to act on it. We need to learn to speak to ourselves in a much more positive way, fully trusting that it works and then follow through with enthusiasm. If you choose or want to, you will find words that work for you and empower your life.

Withdrawal from Fear

Fear is just a word, but it can hamper and weaken the strongest individual because of just one regretful experience beyond their control. When we authorize bad behavior we give permission for anyone or anything to take free shots at our self-esteem. We could choose instead to be more assertive and confident in our intelligence and competence. We do not have to wait in line to be heard or stay on the sides to not be noticed. Yet we allow fear to cripple us. Our uncertainty and limitations crowd our beliefs and faith pushes fear to the forefront of mind. Fear is a terrible existence at any age, gender, in a relationship, rich or poor. Often this fear comes from a sense of denial, meaning you don't believe you are worthy enough to be fortunate or satisfied. When addressing the essential problem it means looking beyond the scope.

> *The weak can never forgive. Forgiveness is the attribute of the strong.*
>
> Gandhi

Discovering what lies underneath the many layers is recovering the signs to the hidden and most significant answer. We are our own worst enemies because of negative mental talk all due to low self-esteem. We can give ourselves leave of those responsibilities by just letting go of that anger. Being appreciative is also giving our selves permission to be happy. Let things happen as they are supposed to be, rather than over analyze or force things. Saying you are thankful is gratifying and you're appreciative for everything you have, the good with the bad. Never be enticed to things you must or need. Simplicity and the price for peace can cost a pretty penny today. Go retain your quality of life with one very costly word and stop fearing fear. Take control of your life and turn off fear, fully allowing faith to lead you to your purpose.

Acknowledge Our True Feelings

Being honest with yourself goes hand in hand with self-forgiveness. Without both, we cannot acknowledge our true feelings and move forward to fulfill our purpose. Every person feels and responds differently and has their own truth. If you know and embrace how you feel you can provide healing through forgiveness.

Affirmations are acknowledgments, and very important to convey your feelings and how they affect you. Sometimes we can suppress a sensation, and bottle up those feelings. Years later they pop up and those feelings may have adverse effects. Taking the time to revisit the past and our choices to reorganize those emotions can clear the way for us to heal, let go of harboring thoughts and expectations this is forgiveness within.

If the knowledge of what you feel is not obviously bubbling at the surface, there are other applications that can be used. Once again journaling, or writing down thoughts and beliefs can provide an outlet to help us acknowledge what we really feel. Another alternative for delving into our true feelings is seeking a confidante, someone that can be trusted to explore our inner belief system and decipher your true feelings, desires and passion.

Free Yourself from Your Past

Learning to disconnect from negative patterns is the greatest thing you can do for yourself. Breaking away from your echoes or someone else's words, things that have been memorized only to bring hurt, broadcasting your business one more time all needs to stop. Calling out dysfunction and all that came with it. Give yourself the permission to walk away from the departed and obsolete so you may live with the living. This will empower you and set you free from things and people that have brought pain or threat. Break through from who hurt you or from the assumptions of your past by forgiving the people, places and things that are causing you to be hung up on the past. Moving forward requires focus on new goals, passions and challenges.

Retaining Quality in Your Life

When you examine something so important as the quality of your life, do you ask yourself was it just imagined? OR was it something you've done or perceived that brings the inquiry? Understanding the broader awareness is the principle that affects our perception and behavior. What come from experiences are impressions that are deeply pressed in our minds and hearts. Any distortions can lead to anger or fear. The act of pardoning someone for something impolite, or even yourself, leads to forgiving quality, even the most unforgivable takes understanding of oneself and compassion for a better life. Releasing yourself and the indulgence of punishment is excusing yourself from the drama.

Freeing yourself from drama and conflict allows you to rediscover and retain positive attributes and quality moments return. Once you have chosen forgiveness and begun to move forward through the process, the focus solidly remains on finding an individual passion or yearning and developing or encouraging it. The excitement of a passion, especially one in honest alignment of personal goals, is often enough to keep the mind focused on the quality of life and the blessings herein.

Change Your Feelings

When we want to amend our lives, we first need to address our feelings. Clearly in order for something to change, you must acquire the wisdom of that knowledge. Investigating something deeper within you about feelings one may consider to be unfavorable, because of the awkwardness of the truth. Being truthful with your feelings is the power to perceive with physical feeling and with mental impression. Concentrate on quality and encourage useful words to ourselves, rather than berating unhelpful thoughts. In this way we will retrain our way of thinking and be giving advantage to our valuable life. Just fine-tune what you already have.

Start with small steps to change on feeling. Pick a negative feeling that causes great hurt and has the potential to prevent you from moving forward, i.e. "I hate him". For a moment, focus on the words, the feelings and why you feel that way, remembering the hurt, the broken promises and betrayal. Then change it to something positive. Anything. It could be, "I am grateful for our children." Or "He helped me learn to be successful." Or even, if nothing else, "I have learned not to have negative people in my life". Now every time the negative feeling (and phrase associated with it) comes up, forcefully replace it with the positive phrase and focus on those feelings instead. Do this consciously, trying to smile and change the feeling to a more positive one. By practicing this exercise (daily if possible), you will begin to change your feelings, which will change your attitude and your life. ❖

COURAGE

Life's Credit Electing What is Good

In our very simple lives, we may have a couple humble opportunities when we voice an opinion, or abstract thought like "oh that's great!" Or "that's very bad!" Unfortunately, one issue we will have is we will be opening ourselves up for argument and there's a chance of resistance that might make us impervious to change or unwilling to be honest in future encounters. When sharing an opinion, there's a responsibility and loyalty to ourselves that we stand by what we believe or think. I can appreciate public opinion and debate, as much as the next, but the quality to be brave enough to share your heart takes tremendous energy and courage. Never be set back by limitations. The world is your oyster.

Have courage by electing what is good, not what is popular. It may be easier in the moment to agree but easy does not equate to good or right. In the end, standing true to you opens up unlimited possibilities. Doing right is not only good for your soul but also is a quick lesson in being respectful to others.

Understanding the Way You Think

If we permit opinions of others to influence our thinking we are intentionally concerned with something that is not necessarily valid, useful or positive. Are we keenly aware that we are allowing others to muddle with our way of thinking because of what they believe? Interference can only bring disturbance and undesirable feelings to our self-esteem and it needs to stop as you may experience rejection and all that goes with any negative incident. If you think about it, serenity is composure of quietness and the ability to plan or alter all unhealthy and adverse language to a more pleasant interchange in dialogue.

Unfortunately because we are taught from an early age to listen to external teachings and beliefs, our knowledge of ourselves is limited. It is possible and necessary to delve deep and uncover these hidden truths. It is only by understanding the way we think as an individual that we can begin to forgive ourselves. This process, the simple undoing of perceived thoughts and beliefs can be achieved through meditation and prayer.

Our Presumption

Communication is almost always difficult because we as humans make it that way. When anyone addresses us, we take thoughts and meaning through our belief system and examine what was mentioned. All this is processed through our own point of view. From there we cast judgment. What if we clearly didn't understand what the other person said, and later the other party said to you, "I already told you that, remember?" Or, "that's not what I meant." We all have experienced plenty of situations as early as a child in school on the playground when we witnessed an event and we all remember a different version of an incident. Often we may ponder if we were the only ones that actually saw or heard the event or how someone's perception can be so totally different than your reality.

Perception is reality and the difficulty is that each human has a unique perception and therefore see every situation from our individual understanding, upbringing and value system. Take for example a person stealing food to feed their family. The store owner that was stolen from sees the situation as a thief trying to hurt their business; that is a personal threat. A well off customer may see a disgusting low-life and judge that person as lazy. To his family, he is a hero for bringing the sustenance they need and to a follower of God the person is another of God's children.

To complicate the subject of concern further we know that people don't always mean what they say. Either they don't want to hurt someone, are afraid of judgment or retaliation or they say it for the wrong reasons. Listen to the emotional quality of the conversation for the reason and emotions behind the words. Listening is imperative as is striving to be present in the moment, not absent. There's an art to listening and being present. Forgive ourselves for not being willing to listen objectively when others speak to us, because we don't agree with them. Forgiveness means not distorting the truth, their words and not ours, interrupting their opinions, or making assumptions what they say or feel. And the same goes for us, where we forgive them for the same. This takes concentration. A few suggestions are to not cut someone off, fade away by looking around the room, as you are not interested and finally putting your ego aside and not discussing your story without listening to the other person first.

Being Critical

When we are critical of one another we should be asking for forgiveness for any judgment about the circumstance of which we were not aware. Always know that everyone has the right to relinquish their emotions to us, as we are not expected to stay in the room if they are rude to us. It's also important to forgive all or any previous judgments of others emotional feelings. Past judgments are just that. They are not today. With present state of mind you can let your present thoughts be a reality worth our time and emotional energy.

Being critical of others is a negative waste of our present reality. If we feel in a mood to critique, it would be much more beneficial to turn that introspectively; viewing instead areas we can improve in ourselves rather than what is wrong with someone else. Often if we look closely enough the things we are critical of in others are similar to things we most wish to change in ourselves.

Courage

Audaciously working hard to be the best we can every day because something or someone inspired us takes a pile of courage. How can we possibly move forward if we don't have inspiration, motivation, or for that matter a plan? If we don't go after what we want, we will never see our dreams turn to reality. There are so many opportunities developing all we need with drive, hope and faith. Futures are driven by sensation, emotions, opinions, and dreams and even on a hunch. Whatever the basis we must look with proper sense of value and personal satisfaction that this is a feeling of superiority and you need the forgiveness to have the courage to go after your life today. Forget about yesterday, it's over. Focus on your tomorrows as they hold the beacon of light to your dreams, your future. Remember forgiveness does not guarantee reconciling of people. But it is possible for anyone to forgive, even if reconciliation isn't compatible.

Having the courage to move on to forgiveness is a huge step in personal development. Wanting more, having dreams and taking steps to implement a better life is a tough choice. Through faith comes courage to try to make a life apart from negativity, betrayal and hurt. Believing instead that our passions can lead us forward.

Courage to Be Docile

When we feel trapped or scared is this because of our past experiences that bind us up emotionally. Frightening thought to think we are bound to just one word because of our personal anxiety. How do we break those barriers to an awesome future? Only one way to deal with that is head on with the truth. Face the monster and respond emotionally by taking action in opposition. Favorable conditions await you on the other side of the door, open it and take the risk and face fear for what it is, you may be surprised by the courage you already have because you confronted your distress.

This courage can come in many shapes and forms from refusing to back down to not allowing others to walk all over you. It is difficult to come out of an abusive situation or betrayal without feeling the need to start a battle. The courage to be docile is in moving on from the experience with grace and fortitude. A difficult challenge to say the least. Once you have faced your fear the need to battle wanes. Then, through time, belief in God and focus on self-healing you will come to a joy, an abundance, you would have previously never imagined.

Top 10 Actions to Move to Forgiveness

By choosing one and then working through the rest, this small list provides a quick jump in guide of how to get the process started. It is important to note that these are in no particular order just as forgiveness happens in no particular order. They are simply a sampling of actions you can take immediately that will move you towards a life of forgiveness and affect change in your reality.

1. *Find your passion*

    Knowing yourself does not always come easy. As well, your passion can be hidden under false expectations and desires. Once you find your passion you will know it with your whole heart. The difficulty can be when you have not uncovered your true heart by having the faith to find yourself. Investing the time in yourself to decipher your inner truth will allow your own unique passion to shine.

2. *Prayer/meditation/faith*

    This can take on many different forms depending on your religion, spirituality or faith. The similarities in all belief systems point to having faith in an energy or connection larger than yourself. In my case, as a Christian that is Jesus Christ and God the father who I call upon to give me strength as I work through my own personal journey to forgiveness. Faith is the

game changer from which the most amazing things can occur. Once you embrace faith, surrendering to the knowledge
you have the strength to push through, you will see miracles
in your life.

3. *Find a lesson in the hurt*

Everything happens for a reason maybe an overused platitude
but it holds great truth. In the moments of hurt, deception,
abuse and betrayal come our biggest lessons. It is through
the difficult times where we learn something about ourselves
and the world, community and people that affect us. Find the
lesson in the hurt and use it to move forward into forgiveness
and love.

4. *Stay silent*

Silence as part of meditation or simply as not speaking the
angry thoughts and feelings that bubble up is another path
on the road to forgiveness. There is great value in not allowing the negativity to spew forth. It can be tempting to share
with the world the hurt you experienced especially with false
friends faking concern only to ascertain gossip. Stay silent
and work within yourself to find peace.

5. *Self-improvement*

This one goes hand in hand with many of the other actions
listed here. Self-improvement is the bottom line when it
comes to forgiveness of self and others. By reflecting on our
weaknesses and the issues within us that brought us to this
point we can learn where we need to make improvement and
by the grace of God learn to love ourselves, forgive ourselves
and live a powerful life of abundance.

6. *Say no*

Love yourself enough to say no to the negativity and constant pressure to be what everyone else expects. This one was one of the hardest for me. As a mother, wife and community member, saying yes was my way of helping others and showing I care. However, I came to realize that with manipulation and ill intent, people were affecting my outlook of self, and pushing me away from my passion. Say no to the things that are harmful and getting in the way of your progress. Forgiveness involves setting boundaries and that includes saying no.

7. *Help someone*

Sure I just told you to say no, now I am asking you to help someone. These are not contradictory actions. Helping someone means giving something of you in order to ease someone else's difficulty. In this case I would encourage you to find something in line with your passion to use as a tool to help others. As well, helping others on your terms, or where faith as brought you, allows you to see the connection of humanity in a positive way. We all need help at times and giving help fills our life with abundance and love.

8. *Balance*

Balance is another tricky action. It may feel easier to balance on your head then to find balance in your life. After a betrayal, life is unbalanced and it takes time to rediscover what balance is needed. Everyone is different but a basic balance of work/life, introspection/social involvement and carving out time for your healing is required. Forgiving the unforgivable is a process that may need different aspects at different times. Strictly focusing on balance in a moment that seems overwhelming provides us with an opportunity to answer the small voice wanting more and juggle life's necessities to allow that voice to grow.

9. *Love*

Love is an action that permeates the entire journey to forgiveness. Focusing on love of self first is a way of healing your heart, finding who you are and creating steps towards your abundant future. The love of God encourages us and builds us up, as a reminder to love others as we love ourselves. Moving toward love when we feel anger, hurt or rejection helps to remove barriers that may stop progression of the path to forgiveness.

10. *Acceptance*

As with love, acceptance means of self and of others. Many of us believe outside influences of media, family friends and society that dictate who we must be in order to fit in. Acceptance teaches us that we should all be uniquely ourselves. Once we accept who we are, weaknesses and all, we can put together an action plan that is suitable for the situation we are in and that encourages movement towards the life we want to live. In the same regard, acceptance of others plays a role here to. Instead of attacking inappropriate people or behavior, we accept that those people are choosing for themselves. This takes away any feelings of guilt and allows the betrayal to be seen in a different light. Acceptance does not mean keeping these people in our lives it means coming to the knowledge that they are in charge of their own journey.

It also means having the strength to know when it is time to remove a toxic person from your life. Acceptance begets forgiveness and provides a positive outlook. ✦

CONCLUSION

It occurs to me that we live in a world where forgiveness often takes a back seat to our own selfish needs or the perceived needs of the masses. There are many accounts of unkindness on a daily basis; the competitions, cutting in line or off in traffic, families separated by point of views just to be right. You think these situations are bad enough but we live in a world filled with war, terrorism and the threat of weapons of mass destruction. In all of the above there is a huge need to learn about forgiveness as a whole and connect with healthier people?

Forgiveness is the hardest quality to outline and yet it's the most vital. Forgiveness is not just an act of pardon-me, nor is it the other person harboring resentment. Forgiveness is not that we are disagreeing that the action in question was hurtful or inappropriate. It is hard to forgive and sometimes a challenge especially if the person has wronged us or does not admit to wrongdoing. Rather than looking what is wrong or right we just need recognize that the action was taken in ignorance of our true nature and the action caused great pain and suffering.

Try granting yourself the courage and the will to forgive the people that you love the most. To forgive every injustice you feel your mind. And to love other people unconditionally. The only way to mend your heart is through the act of forgiveness. Finding strength to forgive everyone who has hurt you, even when you feel the offense is unforgivable. To know forgiveness is the act of self-love. Help yourself to love so much that you forgive every offense. I choose forgiveness because I don't want to suffer every time I remember or am reminded of the offense. Heal the guilt in my heart by accepting the forgiveness of everyone I have hurt in my life. This challenge can be achievable if we sincerely recognize the mistakes we have made out of ignorance, and search wisdom and determination to refrain from making the same mistakes. Love and forgiveness will transform every relationship in the most positive ways, giving everyone the capacity to love and forgive. Sharing your heart to love and forgiveness so that you can share your love without fear.

To err is human, to forgive, divine.
Alexander Pope

Being pushed by the ego-mind to actions back on feeling needed, deserved or possessed. Our fear compels us to take action and can be hurtful to others. Moving past judgment, not condemning others, It's just not our place. When we move past condemning others we say we have judged a person's acts or words to be because of a point of view or society. We get stuck over constant judging. With compassion there is responsibility for words and deeds omitted in non-awareness. Forgiveness of one self is about sabotage and intuition, anger and then having to let go. Peace lies in the limitlessness. How we limit the peace we share are answers only we know and only we can deprive our self of anything. Never oppose the realization for the beginning of the day is at dawn of the first light. Denial takes many forms and we need to recognize not to be afraid for what you will be looking for is the source of fear, and you are beginning to learn that fear is not real, but never overlook the effects by denying your reality.

The first important step to letting go is forgiving the unforgivable and taking back your life. ✤

www.ingramcontent.com/pod-product-compliance
Lightning Source LLC
LaVergne TN
LVHW021542080426
835509LV00019B/2788